RISKY BUSINESS

Marine Biologist

Swimming with the Sharks

By

K E I T H   E L L I O T   G R E E N B E R G

*With Photography by Doug Perrine
and Tim Calver*

A   B L A C K B I R C H   P R E S S   B O O K

W O O D B R I D G E ,   C O N N E C T I C U T

Published by Blackbirch Press, Inc.
260 Amity Road
Woodbridge, CT 06525

©1996 Blackbirch Press, Inc.
First Edition

Printed in the United States of America

10 9 8 7 6 5 4 3 2 1

Photo Credits
Cover: © Doug Perrine/Innerspace Visions
Pages 6, 10–11, 18, 19, 22, 24–25, 26–27, 28–29, 30: © Doug
Perrine/Innerspace Visions
All other photos by Tim Calver.

Library of Congress Cataloging-in-Publication Data

Greenberg, Keith Elliot.
    Marine biologist/by Keith Elliot Greenberg.—1st ed.
        p.   cm. — (Risky business)
    Includes bibliographical references and index.
Summary: A profile of Dr. Sonny Gruber, a marine biologist who
has been observing sharks for more than thirty years and who
loves this risky occupation.
    ISBN 1-56711-156-4 (alk. paper)
    1. Marine biologists—Juvenile literature. 2. Marine biology—
Juvenile literature. 3. Gruber, Samuel H.—Juvenile literature. 4.
Marine biologists—United States—Biography—Juvenile literatire.
5. Sharks—Research—Florida—Juvenile literature. [1. Gruber,
Samuel H. 2. Marine biologists. 3. Marine biology. 4. Sharks.]
I. Title. II. Series: Risky business (Woodbridge, Conn.)
QH91.16.G76   1996
574.92—dc20
[B]   95-20196
                                              CIP
                                              AC

INTRODUCTION

The island of Bimini lies about 50 miles east of Florida, across the Atlantic Ocean. It's a warm, relaxed place. During the day, there is little activity on Bimini's main street. Most residents try to stay out of the hot sun.

In the ocean, the pace is different. Young sharks swim about, attracted to the shallow waters around the island. In the shallow waters, there are smaller fish to eat, and wrecks of boats and small airplanes. For some reason, sharks like these ruins. When spotted, the creatures often like to swim underneath them and hide.

Few sharks escape the expert gaze of Dr. Sonny Gruber. Sonny is a marine biologist, a scientist who studies the sea. After more than 30 years of observing sharks, he has learned to understand these masters of the ocean.

When the 57-year-old scientist isn't teaching marine biology to students at the University of Miami, he is at the Bimini Biological Field Station. His "lab" is the ocean surrounding the island.

Sonny runs the Biological Field Station on the island of Bimini.

Every day, his staff members hang bait on nylon wire that they stretch across the water. When the sharks come to take the food, they are trapped by hooks and nets.

A group of Sonny's students observes baby sharks as they approach.

5

Sonny injects a baby lemon shark with a special solution that relaxes it during capture.

Sonny's purpose is not to hunt or kill the animals. Rather, he hopes to better understand and appreciate them by learning more about them. His two most recent projects involve studying what sharks do during the day, and how their behavior changes at different times of the month.

To improve his knowledge, Sonny performs surgery on the fish, implanting "transmitters" that track the animals' movements for 18 months. When a shark is caught, Sonny speeds up to it in his boat. He makes a small cut in the creature, puts in a transmitter, then stitches the wound shut.

On a hot morning in March, Sonny reaches down and grabs a shark out of the water. "Look," he says. "They're like alligators. If you turn them upside down, they usually fall asleep."

After 30 years as a marine biologist, Sonny has become an expert shark handler.

But this shark is different. As Sonny turns to talk to a guest, his staff members suddenly scream, "Doc, watch out!"

The shark has woken up and snapped at Sonny, closely missing his skin. The scientist, however, is not scared. He continues holding the fish, not letting go until the transmitter is inside. Then, the creature is released back into the sea.

Sonny releases a baby lemon shark after he has studied it.

ater, Sonny is asked if he considers his job to be dangerous.

"Driving down the highway to the airport seems more dangerous to me," he answers. "In the water, I'm more frightened of the waves and bad weather that can sink boats."

A shark researcher pushes a tiger shark through the water to help revive it after capture.

Sonny thinks a moment, then adds, "Of course, you'd have to be a fool to get in the water with a bunch of sharks and think nothing's going to happen."

To many people, sharks are the demons of the ocean. Sonny says the word *shark*, comes from *shurke,* an old English term meaning "villain." "In the old days, sharks were considered wild, uncontrollable monsters," Sonny says. "In some ways, they still are."

Despite this, Sonny is not concerned about wandering into shark territory. "I've always felt just as comfortable underwater as I do sitting here right now," he explains, leaning against his boat on the dock.

Sonny observes the behavior of a nurse shark under water.

13

Sonny grew up in Miami, Florida. He spent much of his childhood collecting sea shells at the beach, and visiting the local aquarium. At age 12, he began scuba diving.

In the summer of 1958, Sonny was spearfishing off the coast of Miami. He was chasing a grouper, a large fish, when it scurried into a reef. In pursuit, Sonny followed. What he didn't notice was that the animal had gotten the attention of a larger creature, a huge hammerhead shark.

"The shark came around the reef and it really scared me," Sonny says. "I thought I was going to die."

But instead of eating the scared college student, the hammerhead simply inspected the scene, then swam away.

"That moment was the moment I decided I was going to study sharks for the rest of my life," Sonny remembers. "I'd never felt an emotion that frightening and, after that, I was fascinated."

Sonny has loved the ocean since he was a young boy.

15

Observing shark behavior requires work both day and night.

He studied at Emory University for a few years, then transferred to the University of Miami to study the ocean and its creatures. Eventually, he would become a doctor of marine biology, and teach at the same university.

Immediately after college, Sonny became involved in a project that examined the mechanics of shark hearing. Another time, he studied the way sharks age. His studies showed him that some of these fish could live more than 80 years!

One of Sonny's longest studies had to do with exploring shark vision. "The Navy was curious about whether sharks could see in color," he says. "They noticed that when pilots had crashed in the ocean, sharks had eaten the ones wearing orange jump suits, but not the ones in green khaki."

A small electrode is implanted in the heart of a tiger shark to monitor heart rate.

Up until this time, scientists believed that sharks saw only in black and white. But, after investigating for years, Sonny discovered that the creatures could indeed see in color.

More importantly, through observing sharks so closely, Sonny learned how to "communicate" with the fish. "I saw that sharks learn about ten times as fast as rabbits and cats do," he said. "Nobody knew this before—they thought that sharks were just stupid eating machines. But I grew to respect sharks because they can learn quickly, and remember things."

Sonny uses a monitor to observe the heart rate of a tiger shark with an implanted electrode.

19

Name any of the world's 250 or so species of sharks, and Sonny can come up with a quick description. Lemon sharks are "easily trained. They can swim through a maze if you set one up." Blue sharks are "elegant, open-ocean swimmers." Tiger sharks are "the garbage cans of the sea. They'll eat anything." Hammerheads "have highly developed senses." Makos are "the fastest sharks. They jump high."

The dreaded Great White shark is descended from the now-extinct Great Tooth. "In prehistoric times, the Great Tooth grew as large as a bus," Sonny says. "Today, the Great White is the largest predator shark. It's located everywhere in the world. They can be found off Miami Beach or Nome, Alaska—just like humans."

A tiger shark.

At right: A Caribbean reef shark.
Below: A sharpnose shark.

An underwater film-maker gets in close to catch a lemon shark giving birth.

Although Sonny likes sharks, he also realizes the animals won't always return his affection. "You always have to be careful," he says. "Any animal with 300 teeth—and they're all sharp—that's dangerous."

Once, Sonny brought a television crew into the ocean near the base in Bimini. The scientist hung shark food—or "chum"—from his boat, and, soon, the sharks appeared. For a long time, the animals swam around peacefully, as an underwater cameraman recorded the action. Then, for no reason, a tiger shark turned on the photographer and bit hard into the camera lens, chasing the man back onto the vessel.

"You can fool yourself into thinking, 'I'm a professional. I know everything there is to know about sharks,'" Sonny says. "Then, something like this makes you realize you don't."

Sonny uses a dye to check
the breathing of a nurse
shark he is working on.

Sonny has only been attacked by sharks on two occasions. Several years ago, he was bitten by a small lemon shark as he placed it in a tank in a laboratory. On another occasion, a tiger shark smacked him with its tail.

"It left a scar on my leg," he explains. "You see, the scales on a shark are called dermal denticles. That means 'little teeth.' The skin of a shark is actually plated with thousands of sharp little teeth. When sharks attack people, they may bump them first and cut them that way."

Yet, sharks do not kill as many humans as most people think. "We hear about 30 shark deaths a year," Sonny notes. "How many deaths do humans commit a year? Millions. Still, people are scared to death of these animals."

Sonny opened the Bimini Biological Field Station, on one of the 700 islands of the Bahamas, in 1990. Among his goals: educating others about sharks. Every year, the lab receives visits from college students, scientists, and journalists from all over the world. An essay contest is also held at Miami high schools, with winners receiving trips to the island.

Researchers from the University of Miami pull a captured blacktip shark up to their boat for observation and measurement.

"Children love dinosaurs, dolphins, whales, and sharks," Sonny says. "Or maybe I should say they love to hate sharks. If someone is stomped to death by an elephant, no one turns against the elephants. But if a shark kills somebody, it's headline news. Fortunately, things are changing. The more people know about sharks, the less they hate them."

 A tiger shark gets tagged by a marine biologist from the University of Hawaii.

Sonny marks a young lemon shark for later identification in his field studies.

For Sonny, these fascinating sea creatures have only provided him happiness. "What a life I've had," he says. "I have my own research laboratory. My wife stays here with me, and I've been able to take my whole family to some of the most interesting places in the world. And it's all thanks to the sharks."

At the end of a long day, Sonny and his wife, Mari, cook dinner for the staff.

31

FURTHER READING

Arnold, Caroline. *A Walk on the Great Barrier Reef.* Minneapolis, MN: Lerner, 1988.

Cerullo, Mary M. *Sharks: Challenges of the Deep.* New York: Dutton, 1993.

Mariner, Tom. *Oceans.* New York: Marshall Cavendish, 1990.

Morris, Dean. *Underwater Life.* Austin, TX: Raintree/Steck-Vaughn, 1987.

Robson, Denny. *Sharks.* New York: Franklin Watts, 1992.

Seymour, Peter. *What Lives in the Sea.* New York: Macmillan, 1985.

INDEX